LICORICE

LICORICE

Liz Bruno

atmosphere press

Table of Contents

III.

IV.

I.

Admit something:
Everyone you see, you say to them,
"Love Me."
Of course, you do not do this out loud,
Otherwise someone would call the cops.
Hafez

Love isn't the work of the tender and the gentle;
Love is the work of wrestlers.
Rumi

In Montana, I Learned to Not Horse Around

In my state, the cowgirls were queens.
Crowns rode their heads and jewels rode their fingers.
Crosses dressed their necks. They sparkled and dangled.
Men whistled as they walked by softly.

All those ladies got one chance at dignity.
They had one shot to pick out a fine bull
and ride him into the public ring. When he launched,
they held in their knees and virtues tightly.

At least, that's what I learned in Sunday School.
Winners avoid tight tops and loose morals.
They grin, but never make a scene.
Good girls ride hard and stay clean.

Yes, they taught us to keep our lassos coiled up.
Don't toss your ropes out prematurely.
They taught us to keep our legs crossed at the ankles
and hang our best clothes in closets, waiting.

We didn't dirty our boots or fiddle with our spurs
in private in the evenings. We came
when the dinner bell rang and went to sleep early.
We climbed into bed. We closed our eyes and hopes politely.

Chopin and Nudity

I don't want to play the piano if I can't be beautiful.
Frankly, I don't want to touch those keys
if no one is savoring me.

Keep those ivories silent
if you please
unless, through the wall
the neighbors' ears start to sing.

If they don't stop eating their dinner,
setting down their flatware,
laying down their forks and forgetting
        every flavor but my heart,
I would rather let dust weigh down this lid.
I would rather play nothing.

If they don't reach for their phones
to call their colleagues
with the hope that they too
could catch strains of my liquid sunlight,
I'd rather let my fingers grow rusty.

I'd rather attempt 6 bars of Chopin
at midnight with the drapes drawn
so the blind hour can cover me.

At that hour, I can count on other night owls
to sing out other things.
I can rely on the woman in 4B to croon
when her boyfriend is visiting.
I can count on the whole complex
to lay awake, groaning.

Let her be naked and not me.

I Have Named the Kitchen Sink After You

I have named the kitchen sink after you
and the handle of the back door.
Both are thick with the sweat of our palms.

You and I laid last night split like the Red Sea.
Our words walked freely to the other side.
We discussed tomatoes - the wet, redness of their flesh
and the cages required to help them to rise.

We ate warm cheese. I watched the Brie
give into gravity. She fell out of her thick skin
and I understood the word jealousy.

This morning, the sink is full of you.
Our crumbs and fingerprints are stuck on the cups
and plates I should be washing clean.

I can't seem to pick up the sponge.
I can't seem to erase your lip prints
from the rim of the glass, to stop
walking my eyes across the trails
your body left for me.

Jesus, The Original Disney Princess

After you finish that quiz
revealing what Disney villain your mother is,
think of Jesus. (No, seriously.)
Think of that man who paved the road
for the heroes and villains you love today.

He was born in a barn. That baby
was so beautiful and kind
that a crowd gathered to him magnetically.
A star fell to its knees.
Animals bowed to his royalty.

They say that man glowed: goodness danced
in his eyes and love hung off his lips.
Mercy waved in his hair
and gentleness walked in his feet.

At least, that's how people paint him.
They show him in dazzling robes of white
as he rises through the sky - shattering
glass ceilings on the way.

Yes, Jesus was the nicest, cleverest
queen the world had ever seen.
He started a peasant, but people knew:
He would blossom like a mustard seed.

Yes, Jesus ascended. He sits on the throne
beside the King. It's his rightful place.
He had a clean heart from day one
and then his death was kissed away.
True love saved the day.

No wonder girls still tape him to their walls.
His smile is a mirror they hold to their faces.
They dream of how sweet and true he was.
He rose above his life so gracefully.

Skinny-Dipping

If today were forever, I would call you God
But since today is just today,
And you are just you, I will call you mine.

I will close my lips
And push them into yours,
Feeling our heavens collide.

I will walk through the night with you,
Climbing our favorite trees
Like angels who can't touch the ground.

We wander the stratosphere
And shake off our gravity.
We let our wings float down.

Up here, you show me your throat -
The sore war room in your chest
Where angry soldiers stomp and scream.

And I show you my lungs -
The walk-in closet where all my
Disguises are hidden and hanging.

It's metaphysics, really,
You and I stripping things down
And feeling the universe expand.

It's skinny-dipping, really
Undressing in someone else's mind
And swimming around.

To Market

There is so much to buy at a wedding
and so much to consume.
I sample bites of wedding cakes
and taste reality coming through:
I must be delicious too.

At home, I scrutinize my thighs in the mirror.
Can I make you palatable?
I beg my hips to look appetizing soon,
to be mouthwatering so friends and relatives
will bring their forks and knives to the pews.

My fiancé laughs when I suggest
Adam Smith be an honorary guest, but I warn him:
watch for that economist's invisible hand
to write the invitations for our parents soon.

I pick out a white strapless dress.
I hire a tailor to hide my faults,
to disguise them under folds of fabric
falling tenderly like the moon.
Can I be an angel?
Her needle rises and falls.
I tell her I'll wane soon.

I know I must follow the law of supply and demand:
The less of me, the more allure.
It's the economy of female bodies for a seamstress
and it follows old, familiar rules:
diminishing marginal utility
is truth for capitalizing waistlines too.
Less is more and more is less.
Almost nothing is the golden rule.

I tell my saddle bags they are doomed.
When they whine, I remind them:
reducing is what Americans do.
We slash prices, cook times,
and cholesterol.

At the gym, my trainer yells,
This is still the land of can-do.
Pick up those kettlebells and push through.

He says I'd be surprised
what brides will pay to become
as hard and firm as a statue.
They come in wanting to be as slim
as a coin, to roll down the aisle
with a smile stamped in place, eternal.

Beware the Hurricane. And the Honeymoon.

There are dishes in the sink from breakfast and lunch.
We can't recall who ate what.
The bowl? The juice glass? The grapefruit spoon?
They are echoes from our mouths
we already forgot.

I can hardly remember my lips
when they are not being touched.
I have stopped sensing
where my skin ends and my wedding band begins.
They have swallowed each other up.

This house is an eggshell,
all closed up and warm.
We look into each other's eyes
and forget anything else.

For now, we're happy to stay put.
We're fine with dust gathering on the blinds
and dirty laundry cascading out of our closets.
We're fine spending the night chopping carrots and onions,
spinning around each other in the kitchen
like clothes dancing in a washing machine,
whirling into one blurring lump.

Boy

He is lean and firm, as thin and cool as a razor blade.

I watch him study his face in the bathroom mirror.

He is a man, he thinks, when he wears a beard.

He is a boy, he thinks, when his cheeks are clear.

I've seen him fight a dozen battles with his face this month.

He wars with each man that presents himself.

He mowed down the general with the sideburns

And the rakish admiral with the curled-up moustache.

He cuts these men down with a flick of his wrist.

He drowns them in the faucet's drip.

He looks up, ready to fight who's coming in next.

Cut from a Different Cloth

In the beginning, I had no idea
that sweater was a sin.
I had no clue I was wearing a transgression.
I was just a spring chicken then,
22 years old and green behind the ears.
I was always picking the wrong clothes
in the wrong colors for the wrong occasion.

He did not like me wearing maroon
to dinner with friends. He did not like that I saved
broken hangers and tried to repair them.
It was too strange to be lovely, and by "too strange,"
of course, I mean low class. Plebeian.

I let him buy me better clothes.
I walked into restaurants with napkins folded
like swans. I swam away in those middle class Edens.

I began to read clothing tags like tea leaves.
I could discern the future: what praise or condemnation
would come from the church of WASP decorum.

Eventually I could spot disdain,
his parents saying "Olive Pit" instead of
"Olive Garden" or "coldslop" instead of
"coleslaw" with a quicksilver grin.

I learned what to avoid:
chain restaurants and clearance bins.
I learned to hate polyester
and her cheap feel on my skin.

I learned to love crisp dresses hanging
in my closet. I let them slide over my bumps.
I let them repent each morning. They stood silent
as the sun rose. They prayed stiff under the iron.

Pilgrimage

Outside after midnight,
my bare feet lick the tears off the grass.
I wonder how long earth has been weeping all over herself.

I wonder if anyone will see me out here
taking this nocturnal flight.
My thin nightdress confesses my delicate state.

I am not surprised to see sirens careening down the street.
I am not surprised to find other pilgrims
out here seeking answers tonight.

Are you alright ma'am?
Ma'am? Your neighbors called.
Be honest ma'am. Are you safe? Are you alright?

I play my favorite role
for someone poised in flight.
I clench the olive branch in my lips and keep my chin tight.

I play the priest who blesses what they touch.
I say, *We're still newlyweds.*
He's just getting used to having a wife.

This satisfies the officers.
They eat this bread and drink this cup.
They tuck away their pens and say goodnight.

I am left with the front door ready to swallow me.
The old metal hinges squeak in hungry delight.
I lift my nightgown, tiptoe up the esophagus, and gulp.

Two stories above, our love nest
is now garbled with objects: chunks of broken dresser
and strewn clothing everywhere I step.

I know we will never discuss my flight.
We will not speak of the furniture he's flung
or what I fear the neighbors have caught.

He will roll over and turn out the light.
I will curl and face the other wall.
My mind will pilgrimage east the rest of the night.

My Picasso

I'd never had a lover
and now I have two. Maybe three.
They sleep on the right side of the bed.
They wear almost nothing.

Sometimes, at dawn,
I am unsure whose face is facing me.
Whose lips are breathing? Whose hand
is wearing our wedding ring?

One man has big, celebrity eyes
and a laugh that wins people over easily.
He's my lover on sunny days
when neighbors' eyes walk free.

The other man has eyelashes
as long and black as whips.
He slaps them down when our blinds
slide down and the crowds leave.

They are divine, most of the time,
these men in the man living alongside me
or at least that's what I say when I am asked
how married life is treating me.

Only one friend suggests I am naive.
He says golden smiles are never
what they seem: I am still a country girl.
I wouldn't know Zeus if he threw lightning at me.

I say, perhaps, but how long did I wait
to find my heavenly thing?
Now I walk with my Picasso,
my cubist masterpiece, down the street.

I admit, the anatomy of this man
is a puzzling, head-scratching thing.
I am surprised by the shifting faces
that keep rearranging on his body.

There are invisible mouths that rise
and begin to speak. There are extra pairs of hands
that grow up from his torso on dark nights
I see slip out to do their own detached thing.

It's strange to sit in a restaurant and not know
who's holding the fork across from me.
Will he laugh or scream? Will he tornado out
if a napkin or a word is folded incorrectly?

Will I finish my dinner with the candle? Pay the bill
with a blush and a 40% tip that apologizes for me?
Will I walk home in the dark and wait outside the window?
Watch to see which face would turn its eyes on me?

Secrets I

Shall we talk about my breasts?
Just kidding. I jest.
They are perfect, so there's nothing to discuss.
These breasts are so nice they compliment themselves.

However, if my private things interest you,
Don't give up just yet. There will be other chances.
There are things to say that will require me
to unbutton my shirt and undress my chest.

Would you like to hear about the red wall
that taught me the secrets of the universe?
She said I could be Moses
and she would be my burning bush.

On Maslow's Hierarchy of Needs
that bedroom wall was the bottom rung. Number 1.
When I found myself being shoved up against her
I laughed like a tulip giving birth.

Have you guessed what happened next?
If not, please don't be upset.
You know, Moses made frogs and locusts appear
but no one guessed what happened next.

Pharaoh was on his knees weeping
before he understood: the vulnerable burn up.
The vulnerable feel lightening in their spines
when they get pushed. Sometimes, even their lips are struck.

Savior

If at age eight I had been aware that my quiet mother
and bootstraps father could have seen my greatness
as it stood, I might have saved myself. I might have
laid down my rocket aims and grown up.

I might not have spent such long hours awake
holding the ballooning hope
that I could lasso home the loose ends of the world
or weave world peace with a crochet hook.

I might have skipped writing fanfiction by flashlight:
She melts the cold dictator's heart with warm expressions
and precise research. She thaws the Cold War
with her blazing eyes and her well-tailored business suit.

I might have stopped trying to extinguish forest fires
with my bare fingers pushing down like cigarettes,
or stopped trying to hold back coming hurricanes
with just my naked hands and my thighs flexed.

Rite II

I had not been to the spa before.
I had not entered this shrine,
this holy of holies where American women
are reborn and become whole again.

I had not laid on this altar with my eyes
closed but I am told it is Heaven:
God's touch walking in, descending
before or after lunch.

They say the divine can whisper
when a stranger's fingers open
and become celestial lips.
Why else would women enter and strip?

Why else would devout girls
leave their unclean things at the door
and sacrifice up their wallets?
They pray to be made clean and bright.

I am here to beg the priests
for a better life. I am here to promise
repentance: no more sugar or gluten,
no more self-indulgence.

I confess I have sinned in thought,
word, and deed, by avoiding the gym
and eating licorice each night.
I am truly sorry and I humbly repent.

The candles flicker and the cleric
begins her rite. She dips her hands in oil
and touches my skin.
All my muscles' ears open up.

The Quietness Never Tells

By the time the sun licks me awake,
my husband is back beside me in bed.
Outside, the Mediterranean Sea
shakes the night out of her system again.

I ask the empty bottles of wine,
the cobblestones on the floor,
what happened the night before.
They do not reply.
They stay tight-lipped and silent,
like all the bottles before.

I ask the spot on the carpet
where I paced the floor bare until 2 am.
The quietness never tells.
The silence just burns.
The floor stays the floor.

I do not know why my husband left
or returned, or why he is facedown naked.
All I hear is a long sigh. I hear his feces
exhaling, lava starting to cool as it slides by.

I ask my sticky legs why they did not
alert me when this darkness arrived.
They just quiver. They are too
ashamed to reply.

I wipe him down. I pull the sheets
into the shower and scrub them clean
to dissolve the incriminating scene as soon
as possible, at least before the maid arrives.

I ask the shower head why this is happening.
Even she does not answer me.
She just opens all her eyes and cries.

The Attic at the Top of my Neck

Inside a blender it's hard to sit tight.
Inside a marriage you get the same result.

I know I am not supposed to discuss such things.
I know my job is to smile and clam up.
I'm supposed to close my lips like a tea kettle
and whistle inside myself.
Isn't that what people like?
Straight teeth?
Hair that's combed and polite?

This is exactly why I have moved myself
to the attic at the top of my neck.
Up here people cannot hear me muttering all night.

It's a dairy farm in here.
It's an automated factory where cows are milked
without human touch. No manure,
just steel tubes carrying
out the clean, white product.

Don't worry.
I visit my legs and arms once a month.
I tell them we need to pay the bills.
I tell them no one is coming to help.
I am always correct.

Sometimes I dream I am Rumpelstiltskin.
I dream I am weaving gold thread out of straw up here
to buy us a new life.

I let my rocking chair brain do its work.
I seesaw back and forth
back and forth
through another night.

It Dusks on Me

I set with the sun.
I stand at the kitchen sink and watch the day
drip down. I eye that lingering star.
I chase her burn.

The world becomes black and white again.
I slide into the pipes and settle in.
I don't want to turn.
I don't want to see his lips
or hear his feet tapping
as his next confession comes.
Two months before the wedding?
The waitress? The weekend
I was in Seattle? Last month after work
in a women's bathroom?

I go to Heather's alone. I laugh,
drunk on something I didn't drink.
I perform myself like a marionette.
I pull my own strings. I dance again.

Later, I come home and pour myself a glass
of water. I touch my numb tongue.
It feels like hibernation.

I study the moon outside the window.
I never know if it is waxing or waning.
I never know if this orb will be bright
or dim. I never know what house I will find it in.

My Critics

They ask me why I forgive my husband
and I explain: "He fixed the dryer last night."
They frown, as if that is not sufficient.
But they are not married yet.

They keep checklists in their purses
of what an ideal man looks like: a tall optimist
with toned pecs. A strong jaw
and a moral compass. A muscular paycheck.

I admit, I once wanted a spouse like that.
At the lake, I scouted shirtless boys
and examined every meaty inch.
I assessed them like ham sandwiches.

Bring on the mustard, I said,
until the night I saw my sandwich hit the dirt.
I saw him run for the ocean
like a river with no choice but to slip.

I ran after him in the rain,
coatless and calling for him to come back.
Barefoot, I tripped through the woods
until his feet began to slow and give up.

When he turned, the path was thick with holy
silence. Breath on breath, lung on lung,
it was a meal I never knew my mouth could touch.
You're forgiven, I said. *We can make things right.*

And we sauntered back like sheep.
I untied his past and took it off him like a bell.
I said, *Your mistakes don't have to lead you.*
They don't have to ring with every step.

I went free then, too,
lifting my tongue like a gavel.
I dressed in a judge's flowing robes
and felt the thrill of the verdict on my lips: *Innocent.*

Multiverse

When I discover the sixth affair,
I buy a gym membership.
I ask my bathroom mirror if my lingerie is adequate.
Should I become a coy doll in straps?
Practice my pouty lips?

When I consult the internet
I find sex appeal is pretty specific.
Who knew there were so many things to shave?
I thought cigarette legs, smooth and long, were the apex.
I'd been ignorant. Naïve, I guess.

I ask the women selling bustiers what I've missed.
Am I living in another universe?
Is this quantum physics?
Should I get every part of me plucked and waxed?

I watch pretty women on the streets.
They are worlds unto themselves. I see
the gravitational pull around their hips.

I can't believe I never noticed men's eyes
exploring like astronauts.
Now I see them wandering the corners of the cosmos,
weaving between the elements.

No wonder women's eyes cut like lasers,
trying to slice their opponents to bits.
Their eyelashes come out like claws,
hungry and desperate.

I buy lipstick for the first time.
I paint landing strips on my lips.
Dock here, the red smirks. *This planet is a trip.*

I rise at five to prepare for hand-to-hand combat.
I buy a Pilates DVD set
and ankle weights.

For penance I get on my knees.
I do push-ups before bed each night.

I look in my mirror and see my blue eyes
becoming dark pits.
Still, I circle them with pigment.
I draw lines around these black holes.
I whisper: *come on girls.*
Let gravity rip.

Swimming Upstream

He was in Alaska the summer
I was a salmon in Oregon swimming upstream.
I laid in bed and twitched.
His ghost whispered
Get out of bed when my alarm clock shook.

I laid on the floor and waited
for my afternoon shift at the Alzheimer's clinic.
Sitting beside a Pearl Harbor veteran, I saw
time was the general who carried a whip.
I played hymns on the piano and watched
I Love Lucy with women who'd lost their teeth
but not their love of lipstick.

Hours later, I'd swim home
limp. I'd tread water in an armchair,
sinking to the bottom of my river brain
until the sun came up.

What is a body? I wondered.
And why can't I seem to move an inch?

I spawned in my throat.
I laid eggs there and told them to wait.
I said: you'll grow your own fins
and eyes when the sun comes up.

II.

But I always liked side-paths, little dark back-alleys
behind the main road—there one finds adventures and
surprises, and precious metal in the dirt.
Fyodor Dostoevsky

My beloved's navel too
Is an eye to the end. The end and the beginning in her body.
Yehuda Amichai

Ringing

Even when I do not wear my wedding ring,
I feel that phantom limb. I find my left thumb
rubbing its absence on all occasions.

My estranged husband follows me to grad school.
He sleeps on the floor of Brian's walk-in closet
and the therapy sessions begin.

He says he wants to stay married
and I say: I can't wear my old wedding ring
and sleep beside you at night again.

This is why I find myself sitting in a cafe
across from a man with a greying beard and a limp.
He extends a black ring box like it is Jesus.

This sparkling saint has been sleeping
in his sock drawer preparing to rise up.
This man looks into my eyes. I try not to meet them.

I don't confess we're buying an apology,
a piece of metal to soothe my finger so I'll believe:
no more throwing, yelling, women.

Later, at the water, I watch dragonflies begin to mate.
The male grabs the female's neck and she accepts,
bending herself with him into a ring.

They fold into angles I don't understand.
Is this a ring of chaos? Or beauty? I ask my husband.
Evolution? He skips a rock and we watch the ripples
ring like cymbals, shaking the lake into singing.

Hogmanay

Bitter cold, bitter drink
with six homeless hours
to wait for the next train:
to walk down dim streets
lost in their own drunkenness.

Except an open door.
We cross the house of strangers
where the warmth of
Scottish men laughing
boils the air up.

An older man eyes
my stiff limbs. He suggests I relax.
He brings me Scotch in a plastic cup
and whispers: *Soften.*
Loosen like a tired rope.
Unravel at your ends a bit.

At dawn, he walks us
to the fog-kissed train station
and we wait for morning. We wait
for the day to give birth to herself.

We watch for the firstborn train
to erupt fresh-warm and clean:
for that screeching hero
to slide in screaming with light.

We watch for her long torso
to push in and head straight for us.
We wait for her many mouths to click open.

In the Hours

In the hours of your birth, they crowded around
with scalpels ready to cut a quick trail,
blades ready to slice a path through our wilderness.
Their white gloves promised a clean, straightforward life.

I laid thick and naked, as wide as a trunk.
I laid coarse and uncultivated as your father and I
directed the men with tools to stand back:
to let us wild ones unfold our lives.

I felt the hard push of you against me,
the slow, agonizing slide of us coming into history
together in the rushing, blushing promise
of your headstrong flowering out.

I dug my heels into the dirt and rooted.
I wrapped my arms around the rails
and readied for the violent yawning open,
the convulsions, the vocal cords shaking into life.

You were a gushing puddle of arms and legs
and cries. You, still chorded and connected,
still chained to me like a pocket watch.
You, the face of new time, being swung up.

The tick of your heart, the racing pace of your breath
as we grabbed greedy and rushed to touch.
Your eager lips chasing me, thirsty for me
and I, just as thirsty for you, drinking just as much.

In the hours of your unfolding, I felt you
unpeeling out of me. You were a crocus cracking through
winter dirt. I felt you sobbing and screaming your life.
Your first cries, my first cries, opened up.

Überfrau

"Man is a rope, fastened between animal
and *Übermensch.*"Nietzsche

I am a different kind of superwoman
with milk in my breasts. Every two hours
I unleash these pumping tommy guns
and save someone's life.

I am a different kind of woman
with this radioactive liquid swelling inside.
I hear through walls. My x-ray eyes
see tiny fists reaching to the light.

I am a different kind of superwoman
caring for this fragile human life. I bound
down the hallway in one step. I soar
and swoop a pleading body up.

Hospital

On the day your father called from the hospital,
I meant to be upset.

I meant to roll down the window of my voice
And sound displeased with his repeat performance.

Why did you not come home?
What was so important this time?

But instead, I heard my voice slip out soft,
Like a balloon floating up.

I found I could still say hello tenderly,
Like an art student remembering Van Gogh's touch.

It was as if I had forgotten, or somehow knew
He would open his lips and confess: *Broken.*

Getting a Grip

We walk to the park without my arms.
They have been lost in this sea of baby needs, I think,
-- drowned in the diaper pail or frozen into place
in the freezer with your teething rings.

Baby, I did not know becoming a mother
would feel like joining the navy.
I did not know I would become such a soldier
or that my body would stop belonging to me.

I carry you strapped to my chest, curling
like a cannonball while I plod on steadily.
I take the path beside the Q River and ask the water
to revive us, to play us out a Reveille.

I ask the oak trees to shake their leaves. *Please,*
use your thousands of rattles to keep my baby happy.
I ask the geese to take their poop elsewhere, unless,
of course, today, their honking puts you to sleep.

I walk us into a state of hush, then sit on a bench
and watch the river. I study the oaks,
standing on either side in vigil with me.
I see their dark circles, their tired skin sagging.

Baby, they are mothers too. They have knots and holes
in their sides where their old arms used to rise
before they went missing. They have stretch marks
and still, here they are standing tall and breathing.

Epicenter

Tonight, I am paying attention.
You have raised me from the bed
and I react like hair feeling a chill:
I stand up in full salute.

I stand outside your nursery door
and count the seconds between your
sniffles and whimpers,
calculating the risk you'll erupt.

I am the seismologist here
and I must predict: How much energy
will flare? Will the surface waves break?
Will even your father be knocked awake?

On nights like this I ask you,
little epicenter, how you came to
shake our whole world.
Why joggle up the block?

Epicenter, I eye the cool glass windows
and feel midnight's long touch.
I hear nothing but the earth's air
cracking around your lips.

House Ghosts

There are stories wandering around this house.
At night, we hear them walking.
Their Civil War feet talk freely.

They sound strangely like us:
the crying baby, the pacing woman,
the man slamming doors shut.

Some days, when you are gone,
I hear them breathing near her closet.
I feel their heat walk.

I imagine them noticing my merits and faults,
observing every act with ghost clipboards
ticking off what's gone wrong and right tonight.

They shake their heads when the baby starts
to scream, so I cluck gently. I make my mouth a harp
and play the house back down to quiet.

I wash the diapers with calm hands.
I wipe the tired house down
until it's extra neat and clean.

At bedtime, I slide in under the quilt
and hear them walking in the hallway.
The loose boards announces each step

By the time your key kisses the lock,
I'm asleep. I don't even notice
that skeleton showing up.

The Woman You Left Me For

She was a twin.
She was so thin you could slap her in a copying machine,
shut the lid, and start reproducing.

That woman was as trim as a cigarette
and prone to smoking them.
You found her mouth and her nicotine
and you lit them.

I met her in March.
She was behind the counter at your café
when I rolled our baby in.
She was selling vegan pastries and I bought one.
I bought everything then.

I am told you lost your job
because of what happened in the basement.
It was beneath the cameras. It was beneath
our feet. It was beneath everyone.

You said it was the alcohol.
But who knows? Your sloppy lips
whispered so many twisting words
I just kept sliding around and spinning.

We sat in the park and I picked grass.
I tossed it to the July wind.
I asked you to clarify why you were moving out
but your response was Greek to me:
there was no *aletheia,* no truth,
in anything behind your teeth.

I dug at my brain for a year,
searching for bones or artifacts
that could explain the extinction.

You lent me her vegan cookbooks
as if it was a normal, neighborly thing.
You walked into our old kitchen with a smile
and you eyed my hips,
declaring I'd grown too thin.

Was that a joke?
I never knew. I suspected it was smoke.
It suspected it was legerdemain:
a skilled magician
diverting attention from where your
hands had been.

I drove past her husband's gas station
and let the whole thing sink in.
It smelt of cheap fuel,
underground and ready to burn.

The police report says
you were arrested outside her door.
They say you screamed and punched for hours
because she wouldn't let you in.

On New Year's Day
you went missing. Chad called at 7 am
hoping I knew something. Did you steal that car?
Break that window? Take the keys from a friend?

I was potty-training our toddler that morning,
caught in pants down
legs out mothering.
Her urine ran down my clothes
while I held her, holding my ear to the phone.

That was when I knew the sexy cigarette
had won. Smoke was in my throat
and all that was left was choking.

What's Left

You box up your last t-shirts
and take your espresso machine
down the back steps. I watch my morning routines
slide into the back seat of a Buick.

I watch you drive east
away from the sunset.
There are no break lights.
You don't glance back once.

I stand frozen at the front window
with our baby straddling my hip.
The washing machine stops spinning.
There is no sound but the clock's ticking.

What is left for me
but this acre of quiet?
The wind sighs.
The trees whisper about it.

Tonight I'll have to find a way
to avoid the quicksand of silence.
This baby will need fresh white lullabies
to hold back darkness' lips.

I will need a tongue.
I will need strong vocal chords to stretch
out like a clothesline, to run long so I can
hang our wet cries and let them start drying out.

I Was Happy to Be His Yo-Yo.

I was content to be dropped and jerked
if I could curl back up to his hands
and be held up.

I loved myself for being the best
screwdriver in his drawer,
for standing tall and tightening
things down.

He needed me at his work party after he left.
I crossed my ankles and my lips.
I fingered my Scotch, understanding
the plan was neat. Be the advertisement.
Good husband. Good man.
A postcard smiling front and back.

The sandpaper and the knife,
I kept them both after he was gone.
They sat in the basement
not knowing what to do next.
Even the can of varnish sat down there.
It separated slowly.
I opened it later and saw my face
reflecting.

Hope, and her Hang-Overs

They say there is a man I can trust.
A man who can heal leprosy with his touch.

At night I lay in a state of half-sleep
Dreaming his magic fingers will show up.

I whisper wild incantations like Macbeth.
I cook up prayers with all the fervor I have left.

In the morning, when my limbs are stiff,
I remember that God does not listen to bricks.

I remember Jesus called a Samaritan woman a dog.
I lick my wounds and play dead for a bit.

When I hear the baby fuss I get up.
I follow her voice. I unwrap out of my sheets like Lazarus.

A Wash

The ocean and her waves comfort me these days.
Even if she rolls off, she rolls back at once.

She is our mother, I tell you.
Or at least a wet nurse who offers us milk.

Still darling, you cry when her waves ride in.
You whimper when she gobbles your castles up.

Every time she roars, you run and scream.
You stomp your feet. You shake and pout.

Little girl, I admit she is wild and free.
I admit, her tongue slips up a bit.

But darling, she is not as cruel as she seems.
She gave us birth. She sings all night.

She is a slow and steady Tortoise:
She can win races with her endless steps.

Darling, I promise that someday you'll stand on this sand
and see the sun painting the ocean.

You won't see a monster, but someone licking wounds,
gathering up broken things and rubbing them soft all night.

Darling, she is just a set of teeth shivering.
She's just a weeping mouth opened up.

III.

Do you need a prod?
Do you need a little darkness to get you going?
Let me be urgent as a knife, then.
Mary Oliver

A beautiful woman looking at her image in the mirror may
very well believe the image is herself.
An ugly woman knows it is not.
Simone Weil

Secrets II

Shall we talk about what happened next?
Just kidding. I jest.
No one likes the slow bits.
We like rockets and car chases.
We favor Panda Express.

Did you know the Israelites were unhappy
when they left Egypt?
They missed their predictable routines
and the reliable bread served with lunch.

They sat around a campfire
and talked about Egypt and its comforts.
They salivated over sheets and beds.
They remembered everything
but the carrot and the stick.

In the desert, they built themselves
a calf of gold. They needed something solid
to touch. They danced around him,
the metal shining and making
their glossy eyes grow wet. They licked their lips.
They reached their hands toward his smooth hide
and slid their fingers, smiling
and pleased by its firmness.

They laughed the laugh of amnesia.
They shook with the relief
of having something to love.
They'd grown tired of chasing
grains of sand blowing loose in the desert.

Precautions

I buy the blue nightgown
just in case a lover might show up.
Then I approach men
like stop signs: I slam on my brakes
when an intersection comes up.

A man from work starts
howling around my house at night.
Everyone knows he is a coyote.
Still I defend him. I say he is a puppy
who yelps and licks because he can't help it.

We go out to dinner and he compares me
to Sylvia Plath. Poems come next.
I meet his sister and the word
marriage rolls under the dinner table.
It was not a butter knife I was ready to have dropped.

I tell him quietly in the cafe that I'm unsure
we will work. I tell him at my apartment
that I'm not ready for that kind of commitment.
His cross-country hands don't have ears.
They continue to run toward my breasts.

I know I'll have to pull the fire alarm
and evacuate. I know he will
scream and panic.

I finger my hair. I feel
my neck for a chord.
I search for the spot on my body
where I can pull myself
open into a parachute.

Platonic Form of a Hot Mess

When you've been living in a cave
you become a slave to the light.
Or so I tell my friends who keep asking me
what my new single life is like.
Outside, I say, the sun is oppressively bright.
A sunrise can blow you over. Summer bites.

I say: Without my wedding ring
nothing feels quite right.
I say: I am a pile of sweat.
I am a rotten apple under a tree
becoming more mushy every night.

They laugh, as if I'm telling a joke.
I laugh back because I'm polite.

To them, my life is some sitcom I host:
the quirky ex-husband who walks in the door
and complains about his current dating life
forgetting how his infidelity rocked the boat.
She says sex can be casual.
But sex always means something, right?
The studio audience titters
and I keep my face straight.

The joke's on the moon, honestly
that I'm still married to the night.
He calls after midnight
and I pick up, asking if he's alright.

I don't tell people I have trouble sleeping.
I never say: I still picture him at the back door
holding his old hunting knife.

Leaving the Light On

Sometimes I suspect I am nothing but a hotel.
My mother stays in my shoulders.
My father sleeps in my eyes.

There are guests lurking
in every floor of this high rise,
even the uninvited ones.
My ex-husband twists around my intestines.
His mother scratches at my throat,
clawing me down one word at a time.

Last spring, I bought a NO VACANCY sign.
I started to wash the windows
and vacuum the floors.
I asked the guests to leave
but their feet kept walking
through the halls of my mind,
tracking mud with every step.

We Plunge

We plunge into the Pacific
and our wedding guests turn to watch.
We are baptized by Hegel and his Spirit.
We are braided into one conscious thought.
We kiss the *zeitgeist.*

Would you believe me if I confessed
falling in love again was easier than getting a passport?
It took a couple of months, tops.
We talked of Freud and Zizek
and everything foreign opened up.
We read *Le Petit Prince*
and I felt the *je ne sais quoi* at once.

We rode our bikes down dirt paths
and watched the river gush itself out.
We grew every kind of tomato out our back door
and simmered them in pans with garlic and eggplant.
We topped pizza after pizza with that warm dish.

We swam out to Eagle Island
and I felt like a fetus,
floating inside something buoyant.

Planting

I do not know who was feeding who
standing there depositing seed after
seed in the dirt. Curved over, my arms
hung low. The sunlight came through
as I stitched the earth, the eye of the needle.

I wanted to say, *I will take care of you.*
I will return with a hose to water you tonight.
But the seeds' faces stared up
in disgust. "We know our mothers
are still digesting in your gut yet."

Planting, we call it,
as if I will really reap what I sow,
really get what I deserve when
I, too, am dust, when I, too,
am fed on these most holy mysteries
of water, wind, and earth.

Men's Voices

Outside men's voices rise like erections.
First husband. Second husband.
I don't care who wins tonight.

I'm sitting cross-legged in the back room,
playing Chutes and Ladders with my toddler,
sliding through this up-and-down journey we're still on.

I'm finally not the one standing on the porch
asking the intoxicated man to move on.
I am not feeling his breath sour the air and push me in.

She's mine too he used to snap when I begged him
to stop stomping and shrieking while our daughter's ears
and eyes were underneath, held out like offerings.

That man breaks our agreements the way rats
break traps: with hunger and adrenaline. His bony teeth
started to shine. His claws began to extend.

I pitied him for being at the bottom of the food chain.
I pitied him for sniffing around outside,
digging for leftovers in trash cans.

I pitied him the night I told him I loved someone.
He pinned me to the kitchen door
and his hands found my zipper.

His tongue cried all over my vulva
and I said nothing, except, *Please stop.*
I walked my brain to the living room.

I knew if I moaned he would leave,
if I played my throat like a flute things would end.
I could be the Pied Piper clearing the streets.

She Gave Herself Good Advice,
But She Seldom Took It

If unspoken anger is a prayer
I'm a monk. I'm Mother Teresa
praying with my fingers squeezing tight.

I'm hiding in the bathroom. The porcelain
in here is thick and white. Mother's milk.
Even that is not soothing enough.

I tell the woman in the mirror there is nothing clumsier
than new upset. My bulging veins strain like a colt's
wobbling legs as he tries to stand up.

8 Months Later

There's a crater in my bed and it's
smoking. I am sitting inside it.
I call Jake and explain: I'm inside
a second empty wedding ring tonight.

My thoughts daisy petal all night:
He loves me, he loves me
not.

Tomorrow I'll climb out. At day-care
my solo body will say: it's just me.
I'm not the kind of woman
who keeps men for long, turns out.

Tomorrow he wants to meet at the bank
so we can peel my name off him.
I'll wear polite heels and click in with obliging steps.

My daughter sleeps one room over.
I sink into this crater's abyss. I try to find
the middle of the bed and the middle of my brain.
I root around for equilibrium's tit.

The Magic of a Body

Justin says: You'll be fine.
Zip yourself into a dress. Sit on a bar stool
and the rest will take care of itself.

Justin seems to think it's magic,
women drawing men out of bars
like illusionists.

I nod and pretend I know these tricks:
casting a spell on a man's credit card
and making it rise up like a phallus.

I smile and don't say:
*You know I have cellulite
and saddle bags, correct?*

I finish my dinner and don't say:
*Most days I can't bring myself to
shower. Seeing my thighs makes me sick.*

Maybe Justin doesn't realize
because he's only sees me when I'm
wearing a well-tailored cocktail dress.

Justin just sees my breasts
and thinks: glowing moons
that wax and wane in outfits.

He sees my legs
and thinks: magic wands
to disappear pants and wallets.

I laugh as we walk to to door and don't
tell Justin: *I know only one magic trick.
Woman cuts herself in half with
one look.*

In Praise of Not Copulating

When the iceberg sank the titanic,
No one cheered.
When that dignified lady stood firm
And the ship broke away,
No one said: Bravo, Girl.

But perhaps we should sing
In her memory,
The hymn she strummed
Into the nighttime sky:
I was here the whole time, underneath.
Did you not see? Did you not look?

On Wishing I Could Make Love to Myself

Oh I do not mean
sliding my fingers in between my seams.
I do not mean gurgling like a brook
or flopping like a fish.

I mean: the ego and the id,
the sublime and the unkind,
my sailboat and my deep-diving submarine.

I mean my basement self-loathing
and my front porch self-love
kissing in the front room.

I mean my breasts and my bra
working together
instead of disagreeing about gravity.

No, I do not mean the 70s.
I do not mean wearing my heart on my sleeve.
I mean also wearing my sleeve on my heart
and recognizing the two-sides of all reality:
The pot calling the kettle brother finally.

I mean all of my selves around one table:
the fat Liz and the thin Liz at Thanksgiving,
passing the mashed potatoes and gravy.
The loud Liz and the quiet Liz together
in the soccer stands while
the other versions kick goals on the field.

Kiss me, my hands say
back and forth to each other all day.
They are always looking for each other
and finding reasons to meet.

I have not found God in coffee.

I do, however, shake in its spirit
when its tongues descend.

I have not found God in semen
although plenty of men
have assured me theirs was
pure and holy, top shelf sperm.

I have not found God at the gym,
although I do shake under the barbell
and feel fire run through my thighs
when I squat and rise again.

God, I say and then I punch my own gut,
wishing another word would come.

God, I murmur in the morning
when the sun rises
and I roll in my sheets,
willing my legs to do something
besides play dumb.

God, I whisper
when I feel the cool breeze depart.

God, I beg the chill.
But it's gone by then.

This Guitar Has One String

Sean invites friends from the gym to the brewery. No one else arrives. I leave after one beer in the sun: after he leans in and whispers, *I like you, and you like me and, let's be honest, your ass is amazing.*

He follows me to the parking lot. *Can I indulge myself?* I have no idea what he means. But my head is a female thesaurus. *Yes. Sure. Fine by me.* His fingers start to squeeze.

By the time I walk through Alex's door, I can tell it like a joke. *How ridiculous*, I laugh so he is not upset another man had his hands on me.

*

It was stand-up, really, the weekend my father called the police. My mother chuckled about it the next day. Men in uniform escorted her out of a friend's hot tub because my father forgot to check the calendar, forgot to read her note, forgot he had given her permission to leave.

She explained this while taking groceries out of bags. She stacked cans on the highest shelf, up and away from me. I watched her back. The tightness in her shoulder blades pulled skyward. *Anger? Angel's wings?* I wondered, awakening to her at fifteen.

*

When my ex-husband stumbles into my dark bed, I let my legs walk me to another set of twin sheets.

He follows and pulls back those covers too. His fingers tighten around my ribs. His confessions are mosquitoes in my ears. I swat. His bourbon breath dragons all over me.

Eventually he snores and I lay stiff. I hear winter roar outside. By dawn, my limbs are frosted in place. I'm still just a stiff blue ribbon prize pinned to him. *College trophy,* he said in Katherine's basement the month after he left me.

*

On Tuesday, a grad student across the table tells our class Levinas' ethics aren't for us. *We're all privileged in this room. We're educated. No one in here is suffering.*

*

His fingers are gravity. The swimming suit straps are pulled down, no matter how often I yank them back up. My hands cover over my breasts, barely.

I stop saying no. I look at the moon. I shiver, like this is a game of teeth chattering Yahtzee. He tells me he's dreamt of this. I laugh like we're rolling the dice. I know how to play along. I know games end when they are complete.

*

On a midnight bus, I'm shaking. I tell Kim that the married man I've known ten years has just slipped his hand into my coat pocket. I stumbled back, even before he asked for a kiss. I looked at his lips, lost sheep out wandering.

Kim's eyes cut. *Didn't I see this one coming all night?* Honestly, I wore such emotionally short skirts around men constantly.

*

I hide in the library bathroom until the stranger asking for my phone number leaves. I read my daughter books and we laugh. Above the sink, I see my mother's eyes watching.

*

You're the common thread, a therapist said at our first meeting. *You're the pattern. The same mountain men summit and leave.*

*

Professor Peppis yells because our seminar papers are too long. *None of you are geniuses!* he bellows, slamming them down on the table. Eight graduate students sit silently.

He was right, I knew. I could not write myself out. I was endless passive voice and a tangled syntax that rambled on. I was too complex. Winding.

I should play myself soft and simple, I knew. I should be a guitar with two chords if I wanted men to listen to me.

The Dirt On Me

The sandbox is a strange thing.
It's dirt, only more polite and pretty.
It's high society. Raised above things.

Sand we call it, as if a royal snake was dictating
his shopping list... *ssand corn ssand carrots*
ssand the little white mice I love ssand
moles ssand grasshoppers maybe...

At six, I let soil slide through my fingers
and I declared myself its Queen.
Bow peasants, I said.
Each grain fell on its face, rolling
down before me.

Even after I gave up playgrounds,
I spent college midnights sitting on a swing.

In the summer I swam in rivers and lakes
and I remembered my first body.
Do your legs do the same thing?
Mine start to wiggle like jello ssand cartoons
ssand my mother slicing a sandwich for me.

Just last week, in a swimming pool
my eyes bowed to the lifeguard,
but underwater my body disobeyed instantly.

My torso waved like a flag
ssand my legs snaked the waves
ssand I was naked again.
ssand I was Eve looking up
and the rest washed away from me.

IV.

When two people are conversing with one another, however,
a third is always present:
Silence is listening.
Max Picard

Si fallor sum.
I'm mistaken, therefore I am.
St. Augustine

When We Can't Be Together

Two days before my 92 year old grandmother died,
her bone-hand found mine. I held water to her cracked
lips. "When we can't be together, we have to still
be together," she croaked. "Do you understand me?"

The oil painting above her bed showed her at sixteen
sitting in a flourishing garden, proud in pearls
and white tea gloves. People said she bloomed big
every year of her life - a begonia every time.

My daughter and I moved into her coastal house.
We slept in twin beds. I made egg salad sandwiches
and served her Prosecco at 1. Manhattans at 6.
White wine at 8 with dinner. Again and again.

She was always a lady, always on the phone,
always laughing, except for the nights she sat alone
in the dark. She waved a knife the gardener found.
"Someone wants to do me in. Who could it be?"

I pushed her through dementia. She forgot winter.
She couldn't recall her own street. "Looks familiar,"
she said when I drove her home from pulmonary rehab.
Her one good lung rattled, asking where we'd been.

Her heart raced as I put my fingers to her wrist.
I searched for her pulse like I was Vasco de Gama,
struggling to land. "I don't know what's
happening" she gasped, her lips wintering.

She was too sick and I was too weak,
I told my uncle. I threw the untrained caregiver
towel in. I drove the coast while she slept.
I let grief put its anchor down.

Did I fail love like it failed me? I asked myself
every night after we moved onto that island.
I listened as the ocean ran around me
on every side. I slapped myself until dawn.

When the end came, I sat in the nursing home.
I looked her full in the face like she was
still the sun, which, to me, she'd always be.
She winked. Her eyes swan dived down.

My grandmother fell into my fingers like flower petals
headed for the ground. Her eyes fluttered.
*When we can't be together, we have to still
be together. Do you understand me?*

The Ghost of Mornings Past

I'm stuck between sleeping and waking
when I hear a man's voice coming from the back yard.
It walks onto the porch and opens the back door.
The kitchen tile clicks like a clock
almost in alarm.

That is the moment I discover I'm made of
cool mercury. I'm made of cotton. I'm just
one of the bed's blankets, flat and silent
and unable to rise to my feet.

Sleep-paralysis, the doctors call it.
Lilith, I say. A sleep demon
as true as old religion and as strange to find lingering.

It was him, you know,
the him I once married
walking toward my bedroom door
breathing like a lawn mower
ready to plow me down.

A sheep before the slaughter,
I thought. A sacrificial lamb.
I could not scream
when he laid on top of me.
I could not yell into his wet eyes
when they looked into mine. *Cocaine,*
I thought, and didn't know why.
I was a frozen mountain,
snow in my mouth as I tried to breathe.

It's all in the brain, doctors say.
A cloud that will lift over time, they say.

While that may be true,
I'd be foolish, even now,
to say he's gone. I'd be lying if I said:
It was nothing.

Collar

I do not know how to button my shirt
with you in London.
Two buttons or three undone?
I cannot decide which doors to leave open.

I loved you the way my grandfather loved calculus.
He sat with his crisp pencil. He looked out the window
and believed he could fix any problem
by pushing into it again.

You left before I could master the art of tying a tie.
We wrapped ourselves around each other
messily for a while. I could never slow down,
never find my precise fingers with you in my hands.

I never learned to love
your green army jacket with the nude stitched on the back.
I could not make peace with her breasts
or the roaring beast she rode across the universe.

You saved her in Asia and carried her
across continents as your companion.
You slid her onto your back year after year,
whatever job or country.

That last time, in Philadelphia, she rode you
out of the room. You turned, but it was her lips
that had the last word as the door shut on things.

A Woman in Love

I
Police dogs can sniff out bombs.
I cannot. I am nearly middle aged and I still can't tell
when a man is a man
and when he is an explosion about to detonate on me.

II
Can you tell the difference between a pillow
and a woman? I haven't met a man who can yet.
Come to think of it, I haven't met an animal
who can distinguish my body from food.
Ants crawl on my skin like it's a picnic blanket.
Dogs linger under the table, licking my feet
like their lives depend on it.

III
When you zip your pants
I am a mouse again, twitching my
whiskers in bed. I am a rodent
holding my shaking hands,
offering my inadequate prayer up.

Rite I

Let's say I walk into a grocery store
and steal a bag of licorice.
I'm kidding. I pay full price
and charm the clerk. But, still,
I eat the entire bag alone on my couch that night.
My cold eyes stare into the unlit fireplace,
full moons seeing nothing
but the endless cool of the universe.
And all this feels like novocaine:
numbness in the mouth.

Evacuate was the word that came to me
after my husband left. And then
freeze came next.

Jesus took bread and broke it,
saying it was his body.
That was philosophy at its finest.
I break my body too, saying it's bread
or wine to be drunk.

I stand in front of the refrigerator's light
like Icarus trying to escape.
I feel the weakness of my counterfeit wings
with the wax barely holding me together
as I begin to melt.

You know what I mean.
You know the hot white lure of brownies
and the sweet pull of donuts.
Scones and pie can sing like Sirens calling to sailors.
I will have to plug my ears
and tie myself to the mast of this ship.

After the Fight

Hotel darkness for hours.
He sleeps on the floor
and I am an hourglass.
My mind runs and searches all night for him.

At 2, when I am finally asleep
his forearm slides in.
His fingertips are the only apology I need.
I unfold into belonging
and nothing is wrong but the sheet caught between us.
I wish it was nothing. Dissolving.

His arms are so long
that he can hold me at a distance.
Sleep is all he needs.
He is not mine and I am not his
and the ceiling is a heaven I can't reach.

I know I am supposed to stay small
and in my own body:
I know I am supposed to ask for nothing.

The night drinks itself.
The trees outside grow their own wings.
His restless legs slide off the bed.
His toes walk out onto nothing.

An Island who Wants to be the Sea

They say that in America we are free.
I say: when I came face to face with a snake
at the swimming hole, I swam away.
Liberty was not my brain's priority.

We were both snakes, in our own ways. You,
rolling the land and water, giving birth to pleasures.
You dragged your crotch across countries
and watered flowers for decades.

I coiled up in my mother's house,
squeezing into the inches between the bed and the wall.
I stayed hidden for hours, loving the tight borders.
I compressed deep into my skin all day.

At the water, when you said you were not in love with me,
I recoiled on my rock. I wanted to slide away.
I studied the two sides of the stone: to the right,
the shallow waters, and to the left, the deep way.

Did I dive? Do you remember?
Did I stand before you and let myself
hope there was enough water
underneath to catch me?

When I tell this story, I will only remember
that the moment my swimsuit slipped off
I knew I had to tie it back in place immediately.
I understood the rules: Contain myself. Be less me.

Were they leeches? The tiny green worms you
pulled from my hands? Two of them latched
their invisible lips below my pinky. Hunger,
I wondered. Is that the reason we attach to things?

Sink or Sloth

In the woods, I am covered with ears.
I hear my grandmother's slow whisper in a shady pine.
Hemingway talks in the grass beneath my feet.
The dusk sounds like his books:
characters who rarely say what they are saying, or feel
what they are feeling, but still scream
the way a forest screams, loud with birds' songs
and crickets' wings.

In the woods, my ears are even larger than my feet,
which is why, tonight,
I hear something on the ground begin to speak.

I pick her up and carry her home
before I realize she is only a rock
under five tangled mushrooms.
They have covered her
with their sun-hungry needs.

Underneath I feel her carrying
the afternoon warmth.
She still burns with lingering heat.

Do I carry her all the way home?
I have trouble deciding.
Do I leave her in the woods? Lay her down under a tree?

Do I tell her we're both turning to dust?
Do I pretend we are nearly home?
Do I just keep walking slowly?

Second Tongue

Don't hand me a menu in Paris.
It would *embarrassé-moi* to attempt to order *dejeuner*
or whatever the word is for lunch.

Don't ask me to show off my Russian
because I only remember Хулиганка
and Бутербро́д - a female hooligan
and an open-faced sandwich -
which, I admit, could still be a Russian novel
if you threw in some snow and blood and guilt.

Yes, this poem is a dirge about the death
of language. It's a funeral for my brain
and the neurons assassinated in it.

Still, I'd rather not end on a note like this.
I'd rather write an aubade — waking at sunrise
with verbs still in the sheets. How many
phrases stayed the night?
Plenty, if memory serves correct.

I don't hold it against them that they dressed and left.
I salute them for being out there today
kissing other girls' lips.

Yes, this is an ode to Loeb's Classical Library,
to those slim green volumes that sit dusty on my shelf.
I run my fingers down their pages
and feel the old college lust heat me up.

This poem is an epithalamium,
a song for an old bride
walking into a nuptial chamber
unsure of what happens next.

This poem got dressed at 7 am
and felt the cool wood of her front door under her hand.
She stepped out and took a look.

It is good, the sun said
and the poem had to step back
because she thought she had become deaf.

It is good, the sun said with such strength
that the world shifted a bit.

It is good, the sun kept saying
until the poem put on her sunglasses
and went to work.

Notes

"Pilgrimage" first appeared in *The Virginia Normal.*

"Boy" first appeared in *Epiphany Journal.*

"Skinny-Dipping" first appeared in *The Coachella Review.*

"Leaving the Lights On" first appeared in *Vagabond City Lit.*

"Jesus, the Original Disney Princess" first appeared in *The Cape Rock.*

"In the Hours" and "Planting" first appeared in *Interdisciplinary Studies in Literature and the Environment.*

"Epicenter" first appeared in *Whistling Shade.*

About Atmosphere Press

Atmosphere Press is an independent, full-service publisher for excellent books in all genres and for all audiences. Learn more about what we do at atmospherepress.com.

We encourage you to check out some of Atmosphere's latest releases, which are available at Amazon.com and via order from your local bookstore:

Big Man Small Europe, poetry by Tristan Niskanen
In the Cloakroom of Proper Musings, a lyric narrative by Kristina Moriconi
Lucid_Malware.zip, poetry by Dylan Sonderman
The Unordering of Days, poetry by Jessica Palmer
It's Not About You, poetry by Daniel Casey
A Dream of Wide Water, poetry by Sharon Whitehill
Radical Dances of the Ferocious Kind, poetry by Tina Tru
The Woods Hold Us, poetry by Makani Speier-Brito
My Cemetery Friends: A Garden of Encounters at Mount Saint Mary in Queens, New York, nonfiction and poetry by Vincent J. Tomeo
Report from the Sea of Moisture, poetry by Stuart Jay Silverman
The Enemy of Everything, poetry by Michael Jones
The Stargazers, poetry by James McKee
The Pretend Life, poetry by Michelle Brooks
Minnesota and Other Poems, poetry by Daniel N. Nelson
Interviews from the Last Days, sci-fi poetry by Christina Loraine

About the Author

Liz Bruno lives in the Monadnock region of New Hampshire with her daughter and their cat, Lake. She is the Head of School at a private boarding school with 1800 acres of land and a small farm.